LISTEN TO THE TREES

haiku and monotypes

Deloris Short White

River Birch

four trunks united
symbolic – strong
a spreading canopy of
of bare branches
curling twisting bark
revealing the smooth core
the heart
of the tree
in memoriam of Russ

a red cardinal perches

listening

listen to the trees
telling secrets to the wind
whisper your reply

I am grateful to the numerous creative artists, writers, and friends in my life for their encouragement, support, and feedback. This book is a result of their insistence that it needed to be out in the world.

Introduction

One can experience loss or grief at any age, losing someone or something close to you. Grief does not discriminate; it can happen at any time. If you lose a loved one, a friend, a pet, your career, your health, your home... you feel empty.

When faced with loss, life's challenges, or obstacles, I turn to nature. Sitting in a safe space, I quiet my mind and engage the senses.

I encourage you to create a space where you can find yourself in nature. It could be in your back yard, in a garden or a park, under trees or a patch of sky. Pay attention to your senses. Feel the breeze, notice every small detail, smell the earth, and listen for the quietest sound. Close your eyes...then, express your feelings and thoughts by filling the empty spaces and pages throughout this book with words or images.

into the dark

trembling in fear
trying to process what's true
shaken to the core

courage

follow your instincts
facing the problem head on
embrace the unknown

journey

self-discovery
pilgrimage of devotion
through understanding

barriers

frustrating hurdles
lack of communication
questions unanswered

choices

what is important
possibilities abound
accept it – change it

pathways

crossroads and crossings
decisions made determine
beginnings or ends

guidance

seeking sound advice
explanations or guidance
leads to more questions

nature's cathedral

in the open air
take the path into the woods
inviting wisdom

reverence

share your heartfelt thoughts
is heaven listening now?
only time will tell

renewal

replenish your soul
under the towering trees
bowing to the wind

stability

steadfast – fixed in place
become balanced and secure
find your inner strength

bearing witness

acknowledge the pain
and a new way of being
accept what is true